Dear reader,

Thank you so much for purchasing this short book. I hope you find it useful, practical, and easy to review.

This book is a collection of principles and best practices that forms an operational playbook for navigating the uncertainties that often surround business decisions. The focus is on delivering value to clients and optimising internal processes, two pillars essential for building a solid foundation for growth.

Growth Mode On stands out for its unique combination of interdisciplinary approaches, providing a complete view of the foundational checklist needed to drive a growth initiative.

Inside, you'll find guidance on identifying the real problems your business needs to solve and uncovering solutions to those problems. It provides time-tested, effective methods, approaches that have stood the test of time.

"Growth Mode On" covers essential disciplines for growth: emotional marketing, business strategy, service design, and user experience. Beyond that, it dives into how to optimise internal processes, understand your clients, and how to grow meaningful relationships with employees and suppliers.

Good luck with your business and stay curious. Trust that by focusing on these principles, the rewards will follow.

Enjoy,
Raluca

Contents

| | |
|---|---|
| How to define your audience | 8 |
| The Customer Journey | 20 |
| How to use emotions to boost sales | 32 |
| Creating a trustworthy brand | 39 |
| Service Blueprint: How to optimise internal OPS | 45 |
| How to create customer value to maximise profits | 54 |
| Growing the business through efficiency | 64 |
| Balanced scorecard and Value Maps | 72 |
| How to lower employees' willingness to sell | 78 |
| How to build sustainable partnerships | 82 |
| Wrap Up | 87 |
| About the Author | 89 |
| References | 91 |

# Introduction: Why the customer should be at the heart of your business

As an entrepreneur starting out, you already know that success doesn't come overnight. You've poured passion, time, and energy into your business, but things might not always go as planned. You've done everything right: you have a great product, you work hard, but the customers aren't coming as you expected, costs are rising, and your team isn't performing at the desired level. The market seems tougher than you imagined. Sound familiar?

You're not alone. Many entrepreneurs face similar challenges at the start of their journey:

Lack of a steady customer flow. You've created a quality product, but you struggle to attract enough customers.

Scaling issues. Everything looks good on paper, but you're unable to grow your business without scaling the problems too.

Team management. Your employees aren't performing as they should, and you feel stuck trying to motivate them and optimise internal processes.

We know these challenges can feel overwhelming, but solutions exist. This (e)book is designed to help you view things from a new perspective and adjust your strategy to build a customer-focused business.

**How this ebook can help shift your perspective**

The tactics in this ebook are structured to offer a clear framework for addressing the most pressing issues in your business. It's not enough to simply have a good product, long-term success comes when your business is centred on meeting the real needs of your customers.

Instead of focusing solely on immediate profit, this ebook teaches you how to build strong relationships with your customers and deliver an exceptional experience. Once you shift your focus toward adding value for your customers, positive results will start to follow.

**Why is this ebook different?**

The biggest advantage of this ebook is that it uniquely connects the dots between various disciplines that are essential for your business. It provides a mix of strategies from:

User Experience (UX). Learn how to understand your customers and create enjoyable experiences for them.

Business Strategy. Tactics for building a sustainable and efficient business.

Service Design. Techniques like personas, journey mapping, and blueprinting to help optimise internal processes and deliver quality service.

Typically, this information is scattered across different sources – some guides focus only on strategy without considering the importance of customer experience, while others concentrate on UX without addressing operational challenges or employee relationships. This ebook combines them all, giving you a complete recipe that, when applied correctly, will make your entrepreneurial journey much smoother.

## How to use this short (e)book

As you go through the ebook, you'll start to see how the concepts presented can transform your business. From improving customer relationships and optimising your team to reducing costs and increasing profitability, you'll have all the tools needed to build a solid, success-oriented business.

## Basic rules for starting a business

When starting a business, there are a few foundational rules you cannot ignore.

## Understand your product

You need to know exactly what your product or service offers. What problem does it solve? How is it better than what the competition offers? What are the real differentiators that make it unique and valuable?

## Find the product-market fit

Product-Market Fit is the perfect alignment between the market's needs and the solution you're offering. You must answer a few fundamental questions: Is there a demand for this product or service? Does it solve a real problem? Understanding the clear answer to these questions will help you position your product effectively in the market.

**Know your customers**

Who are the people you're serving? What needs and desires do they have? Thoroughly knowing your target audience will help you create tailored solutions that directly address their expectations and problems.

**The User Journey: from awareness to purchase**

One critical aspect that many entrepreneurs overlook is understanding the journey the user takes even before they know about your product or company. Everything starts with a customer's needs. They might not have even heard of your business yet, but they have a problem they're trying to solve and begin looking for solutions in the market.

As an entrepreneur, you need to be present at every stage of this customer journey, from the research and discovery phase to the purchase and post-sale interaction, and understand what your customer is going through so that you can meet their needs effectively. If this journey is smooth and positive, the customer will form a good perception of your brand.

**The role of emotions in buying decisions**

Emotions play a crucial role in how customers interact with your products and services. It's essential to understand not just the logical reasons behind purchase decisions, but also the emotional states accompanying them.

**How to build an ethical business**

An ethical business is one that not only seeks profit but also considers the well-being of its customers. In a world where paying attention to customers' real needs makes the difference, it's crucial to ensure that your offers and sales methods respect both the integrity of your customers and your employees.

Following the Kantian principle of ethics, each individual should be treated not just as a means to an end (profit), but as an end in themselves. This means respecting customers, being transparent, and not manipulating them into sales.

Building an ethical business involves focusing on offering genuine solutions and creating a positive experience for everyone involved. This approach will help you build a relationship of trust with your customers and lay the foundation for a successful, long-lasting business.

# How to define your audience to maximise revenue

Knowing your audience is the first step in maximising your revenue. Building a clear profile of your ideal customer will help you create effective marketing messages, optimise your offerings, and attract the right customers who value what you provide. Defining your audience is the foundation of a successful business strategy and helps you create a business that truly meets market needs.

**Who are the people you want as customers?**

It's not enough to have a great product or service. Once you have a quality product, the next essential step is to identify who you're addressing. You need to know exactly who would be interested in buying your product, why they would choose your product over others, and what draws them to your offering. Knowing your audience means understanding what motivates them and what needs they are trying to fulfil.

## What is a persona, and how do you create one?

The concept of a "persona," widely used in consumer research methods by organisations like the Nielsen Norman Group, is a detailed profile of your ideal customer. A persona is more than just a demographic description (age, income, education), it's a comprehensive image of your customers' needs, behaviours, and frustrations. It's a tool that helps you understand who your target audience is and how to meet their needs in the most effective way.

Source: nngroup.com

**Collect information about your customers: the first step to understanding your audience**

Customer research is essential for understanding who your customers are and how they interact with your products or services. Without a solid foundation of customer data, any marketing or product development effort is at risk of being misdirected. That's why the first step in creating personas is gathering data and studying the real behaviours of your customers through affordable yet valuable research methods.

**Why is this important?**

A deep understanding of your customers' needs, motivations, and frustrations allows you to create products and services that better meet their expectations. This initial research is an investment of time, but the results will help you optimise all aspects of your business, from product design to marketing communication. You don't need large budgets for this research; the methods outlined below are accessible and provide invaluable insights into how customers think and act.

## Methods for collecting customer information

### Surveys

Surveys are one of the simplest and most effective ways to gather information about your customers. You can create online questionnaires using free platforms like Google Forms and distribute them via email or social media. In these surveys, you can ask customers about their preferences, shopping habits, challenges, and what they appreciate in a product or service similar to yours.

### Customer Interviews

Interviews offer a deeper way to understand customers' motivations and emotions. Whether you're speaking with existing customers or potential ones, this method helps you explore their behaviours and perceptions in more detail. You can use open-ended questions to discover what they like or dislike about existing products on the market and what they expect from a new product. Interviews can be conducted in person, over the phone, or via video calls, and they allow you to dive into aspects that surveys might not uncover.

**Observing customers in their natural environment**

Direct observation of how customers interact with your products or with competitors' products can provide extremely valuable insights. For example, if you have a physical store, observe how customers interact with the displayed products. If you have an online store, you can use tools like heatmaps to track which pages customers visit most and where they face difficulties in the buying process. This research method helps you identify problems or opportunities for improving the user experience.

**Learn from your competition**

If you're just starting out and don't yet have a large customer base, you can begin your research by studying your competitors' customers. Observe how they promote their products, how their customers interact on social media, and what kind of reviews they receive. Analyse what issues customers highlight and look for gaps you can exploit to offer a better product or service.

**Finding participants for your research**

Even if you are just starting out and don't have a large customer base, there are several simple and effective methods to find participants for your research.

Social Media announcements. Social media is a great place to find participants. You can post on your Facebook, Instagram, or LinkedIn pages explaining that you're doing research to improve a product or service and need help. Offering a small reward, like a voucher or a discount, can motivate participation. You can also ask friends to share your post to reach a wider audience.

Reach out to friends and family. If you have friends or family members who match the profile of your ideal customer, don't hesitate to involve them. Start informal conversations, ask them about their buying behaviours, and the issues they face when purchasing similar products.

Online groups and forums. Join discussion groups or forums relevant to your field. There, you can find people interested in participating in interviews or surveys. For example, if you sell fashion products, you can find groups of fashion lovers or lifestyle forums where you can recruit participants.

Collaborate with micro-influencers. If you have a small budget, you can collaborate with niche influencers or bloggers who have an audience that fits your target market. They can share your announcement or even participate in the research themselves, giving you access to a larger audience.

Direct interaction at events or trade shows. If you have the opportunity to attend networking events, product fairs, or industry-specific events, you can directly engage with potential customers. Here, you can collect opinions, suggestions, and even recruit participants for future studies.

## What are the benefits of this type of research?

These research methods aren't costly, but they have a huge impact on your ability to define effective and realistic personas. A deep understanding of your customers' behaviour allows you to tailor your product, create a better experience, and personalise your marketing messages to meet their real needs and expectations.

This initial research is the first step and the foundation on which you'll build all other aspects of your business, from market positioning to creating a personalised customer experience.

Once you've gathered the data, follow these steps:

Segment your audience. Break down your audience into categories based on behaviour, values, and needs. For example, not all women between the ages of 25 and 40 are looking for the same thing.

Identify emotional and functional needs. What drives them to buy your product? For instance, a customer may be motivated by the emotional comfort of owning a unique product or by its utility.

Describe frustrations and obstacles. What's preventing them from buying your product? Is pricing an issue? Is lack of sufficient product information a barrier? Understanding these obstacles helps you improve communication and adjust your offer.

Create a clear and concise profile. For example, "Ana, 35 years old, IT manager, high income, seeks authentic products and is willing to pay more for quality and uniqueness."

What are your customers' needs and what buying behaviours define them?

Your customers aren't just purchasing a product or service; they're looking for solutions to their problems and frustrations. That's why it's crucial to understand what needs they're trying to fulfil and what behaviours drive their buying decisions. This requires careful analysis of how consumers make decisions.

**Frustrations and problems**

What are they dissatisfied with in the current market offerings? What do they want but aren't getting from other providers? For example, if you sell unique clothing, your customers may be frustrated by the lack of originality and quality in mainstream fashion.

**Buying behaviour**

How and where do they make purchases? Do they prefer online or physical shopping? How much are they willing to pay for luxury items? Depending on their behaviours, you can adjust your sales and communication strategy.

**Why would they choose your product over others?**

A successful product is one that is perceived by consumers as different, valuable, and unique. Your product's differentiators should be clearly communicated and directly address the emotional and functional needs of your target audience.

**The Emotion Behind the Decision**

People buy based on emotion, not logic. If your product provides them with a feeling of satisfaction, confidence, or joy, they will be willing to pay more for that experience.

Who do you want as your customer – and more importantly, who do you not want?

An essential aspect of defining your audience is understanding that not all consumer segments are right for your product. You want customers who appreciate what you offer, are willing to pay for it, and will become loyal to your brand.

For instance, if you're a company producing unique clothing, your clientele will be people with higher incomes who seek authenticity, quality, and uniqueness. They won't be drawn to mass-market fashion, nor will they buy just because something is trendy or cheap.

At the same time, it's important to be aware of the audience you don't want. In the case of a unique clothing brand, mass-market customers who want cheap and uniform products won't understand why your prices are higher or why you don't offer the same model in multiple colours. Attracting this type of customer would be a waste of resources because they wouldn't understand or appreciate the value you provide.

## The Customer Journey. Creating a customer experience that drives loyalty

What does your customer's experience look like from the moment they first hear about your product to when they make a purchase?

Every interaction a customer has with your brand, whether online or offline, is part of what we call the customer journey. This journey begins the moment a customer discovers your product or service and continues through the purchase, and even afterward. The customer experience also includes post-sale interactions, such as product delivery, support services, and the recommendations they make to others.

To have a clear picture of this journey, it's essential to identify and map each touchpoint and understand what your customer feels at every moment. From product discovery to purchase and post-sale interactions, every detail matters.

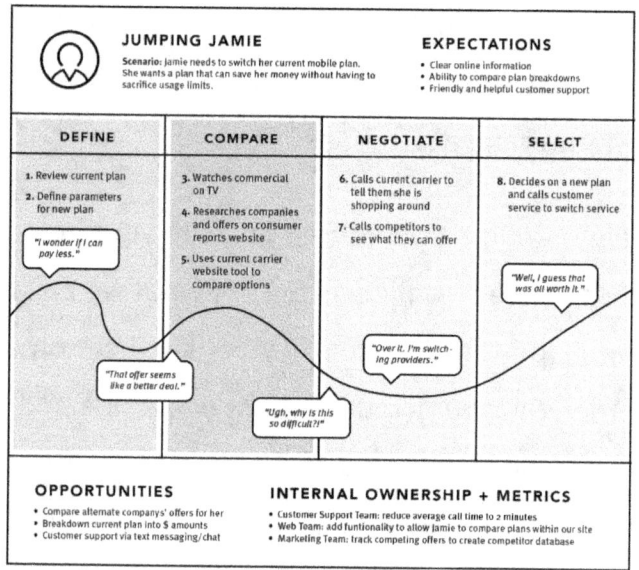

Source: nngroup.com

## Mapping the Customer Journey

Mapping the customer journey is one of the most effective tools you can use to optimise the experience you offer. Often, small friction points a customer experiences are what determine whether they will recommend you to others or return for future purchases.

A Customer Journey Map helps you visualise every step a customer takes and identify where bottlenecks or problems arise. This is crucial for understanding why, in some cases, sales aren't growing or why a customer abandons their shopping cart before completing the purchase. More importantly, this process helps you understand the customer's emotional state at each phase of their journey. Emotions can directly intervene between the customer and a purchase, and managing them is key to creating a smooth and enjoyable experience.

**What does a customer journey look like for a burger business?**

**Discovering the brand**

The customer sees an ad on Instagram for a new artisanal burger that promises organic, locally sourced ingredients and an unforgettable taste. This is their first interaction with the brand and the starting point of the journey.

### Research

After seeing the ad, the customer does some research. They may visit the restaurant's website or social media pages to check reviews, pictures, and details about the menu. At this stage, it's crucial for the information to be easily accessible and create a positive impression.

### Visiting the location

Once convinced that it's worth trying, the customer decides to visit the restaurant. Here, the interaction begins with the greeting and the restaurant's atmosphere. The ambiance, cleanliness, and staff attitude strongly influence the first impression. If the customer is greeted promptly and kindly, their excitement builds.

### Interact with the menu and staff

Once inside, the customer studies the menu and talks to the staff. If the menu is clear and detailed, and the staff is well-informed and friendly, the customer will have a positive experience. Any ambiguity or lack of clarity in the menu could lead to confusion and frustration.

**Place the order and wait time**

After choosing what to order, the customer interacts with the cashier or waiter. The waiting time to place the order and then to receive the food is a critical moment. If the wait is reasonable and everything runs smoothly, the customer will be satisfied. However, if the wait is too long or the order arrives incomplete, they may become frustrated.

**Enjoying the product**

The key moment of the journey is the taste and quality of the burger. If the food is delicious and meets the expectations set by ads or recommendations, the customer will be thrilled. If the product falls short, disappointment can affect their desire to return.

**Feedback and recommendations**

After the meal, the customer forms an overall opinion. If the experience was positive, they may leave a favourable review on social media or recommend the restaurant to friends. This is a critical phase, as a good experience can bring in new customers through word-of-mouth recommendations.

**What happens when a customer has a negative experience?**

Even if, in a situation of poor service, the business still earns the money from that customer, the long-term consequences can be devastating. When a customer has a negative experience, whether it's due to an unfriendly server, a poorly made burger, or the food arriving cold, they will react. Most likely, they will tell their friends about the bad experience, leave negative reviews online, and, most importantly, they won't return.

This type of negative feedback damages the business's reputation and can drive away not only that customer but also potential customers who might be influenced by their opinion. Yes, the restaurant may make some money in the short term by providing mediocre service, but in the long run, the losses are much greater.

A successful business doesn't rely on quick wins but on building long-term relationships with customers by offering an experience that makes them come back and recommend your place to others. This is the difference between a business that merely survives in the short term and one that grows sustainably.

## How to create a customer journey map for in-store purchases

Creating a Customer Journey Map for physical purchases means understanding every step your customer takes—from discovering the product to the physical interaction with the store and the product, and even after consumption. This helps you visualise the touchpoints and emotions the customer experiences at each phase. It's essential for discovering problems, identifying opportunities for improvement, and optimising the customer experience.

**Steps to create a customer journey map**

**Identify key touchpoints**

Start by identifying all the points of interaction between the customer and your business. In the case of a burger restaurant, these touchpoints could include:

- Discovering the location (via social media, walking by, or through recommendations).
- First interaction with staff (greeting and welcoming).
- Studying the menu and deciding what to order (menu clarity and staff assistance).
- Placing the order and waiting for the food (waiting time and communication).
- Receiving the food and consuming it (quality of the product and presentation).
- Post-consumption experience (feedback, reviews, and recommendations to friends).

**Understand the customer's emotional state at each stage**

Each interaction is accompanied by an emotion. When a customer discovers the restaurant, they might feel excitement or curiosity. During the wait for food, they may feel anticipation or frustration if the wait is too long. Understanding these emotions allows you to adjust the customer experience and eliminate moments of stress or frustration.

**Identify friction points and bottlenecks**

As you map out each touchpoint, it's important to identify where problems or bottlenecks might occur. For example:

If the menu is confusing or difficult to read, customers may struggle to decide what to order.

If the wait time for food preparation is too long, the customer may become impatient.

If the final product doesn't meet expectations (e.g., the burger is cold or poorly assembled), this will leave a negative impression.

**Test and optimise the journey**

After creating the Customer Journey Map, it's important to test each stage and see if you can improve the process. You can ask customers for feedback to learn where they face difficulties or what they would change about the experience. This way, you can make adjustments that significantly improve overall satisfaction.

**Why does mapping a journey help your business?**

**You can identifying problems**

You can quickly discover why customers aren't returning or why sales aren't growing by analysing each step of their journey. For example, if many customers abandon their purchase at the point of placing the order, the issue may lie in the menu or the interaction with staff.

**Improve customer experience and loyalty**

Once you've smoothed out the frictions in the customer journey, they will have a more enjoyable experience, making them more likely to return and recommend your business to others. A consistent and satisfying experience is the key to building long-term loyalty.

**Increasing long-term sales**

A positive experience makes customers more willing to recommend your place, come back again, and spend more. While you might make money from a dissatisfied customer in the short term, it's far more profitable to create an experience that brings customers back over the long term.

**Understanding customers' emotions**

Customers' emotions play a crucial role in purchasing decisions. If a customer becomes frustrated or disappointed at any point in their journey, you risk losing them. Understanding and managing these emotions allows you to create a smoother experience and prevent dissatisfaction.

## How to use emotions to boost sales

Over time, research has shown that despite appearing rational, most purchase decisions are primarily driven by emotions. People don't choose products or services solely based on their functionality or price but also for how they make them feel.

Philosopher Michel Foucault highlighted an idea, stating that in ancient Greece, morality focused on actions, in Christianity on desires, and in Kant's philosophy on conscious intentions. Today, the primary "field of morality" is emotions (Foucault, Genealogy of Ethics).

This concept has also been proven in marketing, where a brand's success no longer depends solely on the product itself, but on the emotions it evokes in the minds and hearts of consumers. When you understand the emotions of your customers and incorporate them into your sales strategy, you maximise your chances of building long-term relationships and increasing sales.

## Don Norman's Theory: The three levels of emotional design

One of the most influential thinkers in design and consumer psychology, Don Norman, describes three levels of emotions we experience when interacting with a product or service in his book Emotional Design: visceral, behavioural, and reflective. Each plays a crucial role in how we perceive and decide to buy or use a product.

**Visceral (immediate emotion)**

This is the first reaction we have to a product or service. It is based on instincts and the sensations we feel upon first seeing it: design, colour, shape, and packaging. For example, when you see a pair of jeans displayed in a store, the visual appeal: colour, fit, and style, can instantly attract you. If the jeans have an attractive design and are placed in a well-thought-out setting, the visceral reaction is positive, making you more inclined to purchase them.

**Behavioral (how we feel during use)**

This relates to the pleasure we get from using the product or service. In the case of jeans, the tactile interaction is crucial: you touch them, try them on, and notice how they feel on your skin. If they are comfortable, soft, and fit perfectly, the behavioural sensation is enjoyable. Jeans that offer comfort and ease in use contribute to long-term satisfaction and encourage brand loyalty.

**Reflective (what the product means to us)**

This is the deepest level, where a product or service influences our self-image or social status. With jeans, if the brand represents something meaningful to you, such as sustainability or urban style, they become more than just a piece of clothing. Purchasing a pair of jeans from a brand you identify with gives you reflective satisfaction—they define you, complement your personal style, and say something about your choices and identity.

**Daniel Kahneman's Theory: System 1 and System 2 thinking**

Daniel Kahneman, Nobel laureate in economics, revolutionised the understanding of how people make decisions. In his book Thinking, Fast and Slow, he introduces two modes of thinking:

**System 1 (fast and intuitive thinking)**

This system governs fast, instinctive reactions. It operates automatically, without effort, and is responsible for most daily decisions, including purchasing choices. System 1 is driven by emotions, quick impressions, and subconscious associations. For example, when you see a limited-time offer, your immediate reaction, governed by System 1, urges you to act quickly so you don't miss out.

**System 2 (slow and rational thinking)**

This system governs complex decisions and logical reasoning. System 2 requires effort and time to process information and make informed decisions. It is less involved in everyday choices, including purchases. For instance, System 2 comes into play when a customer carefully evaluates all options before buying a car, analysing price, features, and maintenance costs.

Most purchasing decisions are driven by System 1: fast, emotional, and automatic. Because of this, it's essential for brands to craft their messages and products in a way that triggers positive emotions and activates this quick-thinking system.

**Cognitive biases that influence buying decisions**

Emotions are amplified by a series of cognitive biases that distort how we perceive information and make decisions. Some of the most important and frequent biases that influence consumer behaviour include:

**Loss Aversion**

This bias suggests that people prefer to avoid a loss than gain something of equivalent value. For example, consumers are more motivated to make a purchase when presented with the risk of losing a limited-time offer or an exclusive product, rather than focusing on the benefits of acquiring it. Marketing campaigns using messages like "only available today" or "limited stock" rely on this bias.

### Social Proof

People are heavily influenced by the actions of others. If a product is popular or recommended by respected individuals, they are more likely to buy it. Online reviews, testimonials, and influencer endorsements are all ways to leverage this bias, showing consumers that others have had positive experiences with the product.

### Anchoring

When making decisions, people tend to rely too much on the first piece of information they encounter. For example, if a product is initially presented at a very high price and then offered at a significant discount, the reduced price will seem much more attractive than if they had only seen the discounted price. This way, you can influence the perception of value by how you structure information.

### Framing Effect

The way information is presented influences the final decision. For example, promoting a product as "80% lean" versus "20% fat" elicits different reactions, even though the information is identical. How you "frame" information can strongly influence consumers' perceptions and buying decisions.

# Creating a trustworthy brand that attracts customers and increases revenue

Understanding the emotions and cognitive biases that influence consumers can help you create more effective marketing strategies. However, it's important to apply these techniques in an ethical way, focusing on improving the customer experience rather than manipulating or misleading them.

Here are a few ways to do this while respecting customer integrity and building long-term trust-based relationships:

**Use "Loss Aversion" to create limited offers and generate a sense of urgency, but be transparent**

Limited-time offers are a powerful tool, but it's essential to be honest with your customers. If you say an offer is available for a short time, make sure that period is real. Customers can sense when urgency is artificially created, and once trust is lost, it's difficult to regain. For example, you can use this principle for seasonal campaigns, genuine stock reductions, or special events, but always with integrity.

**Apply "Anchoring" to establish a pricing reference point, but clearly highlight the value provided**

Offering an anchor point (original price vs. discounted price) is an effective technique for helping customers assess the value of an offer. However, it's important to ensure that the initial prices displayed are real and accurate. When offering a discount, customers should feel they're receiving genuine value, not being drawn in by artificial discounts. An ethical approach would be to offer clarity on discounts and explain how you arrived at the initial price (e.g., "Discount applied based on available stock" or "Introductory price reduction for launch").

**Build campaigns based on "social proof" by displaying positive reviews and customer testimonials, but focus on authenticity**

It's tempting to display only the best reviews, but an ethical approach means presenting a balanced view of customer opinions. Customers appreciate honesty and trust brands that don't hide less favourable feedback. You can highlight how you've used negative feedback to improve your product or service, showing customers that you value their input and are focused on enhancing their experience. Encourage genuine reviews and show that you truly care about consumers' opinions, not just the image you project.

**Create products that resonate at the "reflective" level by offering not just functionality, but also an authentic connection to customer values**

Many consumers want to align themselves with brands that reflect their values and lifestyle. To do this ethically, you must understand what your customers are going through and create products that not only meet their needs but also respect their beliefs. For example, a brand that promotes sustainability must ensure that its products are genuinely eco-friendly and that the promises made are part of the company's real commitment, not just marketing tactics.

**Using the "framing effect" to clearly highlight options and benefits without manipulating information**

The way you present information influences customers' perceptions. You can structure information to highlight the benefits of a product, but be careful not to hide important details or manipulate the data to mislead customers. Be transparent about the benefits and potential drawbacks of the product, ensuring that customers feel informed, not manipulated.

**How to create an authentic, non-manipulative customer experience**

When you use these marketing and psychology principles, your goal should be to enhance the customer experience, not to manipulate them. A well-informed and respectfully treated customer will return and recommend your brand, while a customer who feels deceived will lose trust in you.

**A pleasant and authentic experience is based on:**

**Empathy**

Understand what your customer is going through at every step and create solutions that make their life easier and more enjoyable. Put yourself in their shoes and imagine what you'd like to experience if you were in their position.

**Transparency**

Be open with your customers about what you offer and any product limitations. Promise only what you can deliver and keep your commitments. Customers appreciate honesty and will trust your brand more in the long run.

**Personalization**

Offer customers an experience that fits their preferences and values. Create opportunities for personalised interaction, showing that you care about each customer individually. For example, you can tailor offers or marketing messages based on purchase history and customer interests.

**Building a relationship based on trust and positive emotions**

By using consumer psychology and understanding cognitive biases, you can create effective, ethical marketing strategies focused on delivering a positive experience to your customers. Instead of manipulating customer emotions, you can use these principles to better understand their needs and behaviours, offering them an authentic and satisfying experience.

Customers will remember how you made them feel, and they'll return not only for your product but for the experience you provided. In today's business world, success is not just about short-term gains but about building long-lasting relationships based on trust and respect.

# How to optimise internal operations to increase efficiency

In a competitive business environment, success also depends on the efficiency of internal processes that enable service delivery. A well-organised business, with clearly defined workflows, allows you to improve the quality of services, respond more quickly to customer demands, and maximise long-term profit.

**Service blueprint. The key tool for optimising internal processes**

If a Customer Journey Map is focused on the customer experience and traces the touchpoints between the customer and the business, a Service Blueprint is focused on the internal processes that make delivering a quality service possible. It details workflows, team responsibilities, and interactions between departments, offering a clear view of how the business functions internally.

The Service Blueprint was introduced by G. Lynn Shostack in the 1980s and is used by companies around the world to identify weaknesses in internal processes and optimise service delivery. The goal is to improve organisation and efficiency so that the customer receives a frictionless, high-quality service.

**SERVICE BLUEPRINT** *Example*

Source: nngroup.com

## Why is a Service Blueprint important?

A Service Blueprint is essential for understanding how the business operates internally and identifying where problems occur. Without a clear vision of workflows, the resources involved, and how teams collaborate, the business can become chaotic, inefficient, and difficult to scale.

You might think, "it works well enough" without a well-defined plan, but the real question is: is this the type of business you want? A business that relies on improvisation, chaotic efforts, and stress won't survive in the long term. Without structure, you risk burnout, losing customers, or failing to meet their needs efficiently. If you want to grow intelligently, stay organised, and have control over your business, a Service Blueprint can provide the clarity you need.

## How to create a Service Blueprint?

To build a Service Blueprint, follow these essential steps:

### Identify customer touch points (Customer Actions)

These are all the interactions the customer has with your business, whether it's placing an order in a restaurant or receiving post-sale support. This step is similar to what you already have in the Customer Journey Map.

**Document customer-visible activities (Frontstage)**

This includes all the actions the customer can see. For example, in a burger restaurant, this might include taking orders, serving burgers, and interactions with staff.

**Document activities invisible to the customer (Backstage)**

These are all the processes happening behind the scenes that the customer doesn't see but are essential for service delivery. For example, preparing the burgers in the kitchen, managing ingredient inventory, or cleaning the restaurant.

**Map the technological support**

Identify the technologies or tools involved in delivering the service. In our burger restaurant example, this could include a digital ordering system, stock management software, or electronic payment systems.

**Identify barriers and weak points**

Analyse the workflow and identify issues that are preventing smooth operations. These could include communication bottlenecks between the kitchen and the front-stage staff or problems in order management.

**Example of a service blueprint for a burger restaurant (in-store purchase)**

Let's take the example of an artisanal burger restaurant and build a simplified Service Blueprint. We'll detail each step in the process, from customer interaction to behind-the-scenes operations.

**Customer Actions**

The customer enters the restaurant.

- They study the menu and place an order at the cashier.
- They wait for the order.
- The customer receives the burger and eats.
- The customer provides feedback or leaves a review.
- Frontstage (Customer-Visible Actions)
- The cashier greets the customer and takes the order.
- Staff serve the food at the table.
- Interaction between staff and customer: checking if everything is satisfactory or providing menu information.

**Backstage (Customer-Invisible Actions)**

- The kitchen prepares the order (cutting vegetables, cooking meat, assembling the burger).
- The order management system sends information to the kitchen.
- Managing stock of ingredients (checking the stock of meat, vegetables, sauces).
- Cleaning the kitchen and dining area.

### Technological Support

- Digital ordering system for staff (POS).
- Inventory management software.
- Electronic payment system.
- Feedback or review app.

## Internal problems identified in the blueprint and possible solutions

### Unclear or incomplete orders

The kitchen receives unclear or incomplete orders, leading to mistakes in preparing burgers. The customer waits longer than expected or receives the wrong order.

What to do? Implement a more efficient digital ordering system with clear options and detailed instructions for the kitchen, reducing the risk of confusion. Additionally, introduce a double-check system for orders before they are sent to the kitchen.

### Communication between kitchen and staff

There's a lack of effective communication between the kitchen and front-stage staff, causing delays in table service and a frustrating customer experience.

What to do? Introduce clear interaction points between the kitchen and front-stage staff, either through a digital notification system or clear procedures for checking order status.

**Ingredient stock management**

Ingredient stock isn't properly managed, leading to unexpected shortages and customer dissatisfaction when they can't order their preferred products.

What to do? Implement inventory management software that alerts staff when stock is running low, allowing timely restocking and avoiding unpleasant situations.

A Service Blueprint is an extremely valuable tool for any entrepreneur who wants to have a clear view of how their business operates from the inside. It helps identify problems and streamline processes, providing a solid foundation for scaling the business. Without a well-organised internal structure, your business can descend into chaos, where internal issues prevent long-term growth.

If you're dedicated to organisation, efficiency, and intelligent scaling, the Service Blueprint is an essential artefact that will help transform how your business operates and ensure consistent quality service, even as you grow.

# How to create customer value to maximise profits

What is value and how do we define it? Value represents the difference between a customer's perception of a product or service and the cost they are willing to pay for it.

Creating value is fundamental for long-term financial success, and companies that excel in this area manage to create differentiated value for customers, employees, and partners.

Value is created through two essential mechanisms:

- Increasing the Willingness to Pay (WTP) of customers.
- Decreasing the Willingness to Sell (WTS) of employees and suppliers.

These two components play an essential role in building a successful business model. By increasing WTP, customers are willing to pay more for your products or services. By lowering WTS, you manage to provide better working conditions for employees and reduce costs, thus increasing profit margins.

## What is Willingness to Pay (WTP)?

Willingness to Pay (WTP) is the maximum amount a customer is willing to pay for a product or service. WTP is influenced by a variety of factors, including:

- Product or service functionality.
- The experience the product offers.
- Branding and the emotional relationship the customer has with the product.

It's important to note that WTP is not the same as price. The price is the actual amount paid by the customer, while WTP reflects the customer's perceived value and how much they are willing to pay for the experience offered.

For example, Apple has successfully increased WTP by creating a strong brand identity and providing a seamless customer experience, which includes both the functionality of their products and the emotional connection customers feel with the brand.

## What is Willingness to Sell (WTS)?

On the other hand, Willingness to Sell (WTS) represents the minimum amount an employee or supplier is willing to accept to work or supply a product. WTS reflects the quality of the relationship between the company and its employees or suppliers. If employees feel appreciated, have good working conditions, and access to professional development opportunities, WTS decreases. Thus, the company can retain these employees at lower costs.

For example, Patagonia has managed to decrease WTS by creating a company culture focused on environmental sustainability and employee well-being. By offering meaningful work and fostering a supportive work environment, Patagonia has reduced employee turnover and improved operational efficiency.

## How to create value for customers

Creating value starts with a deep understanding of customer needs and expectations. There are three essential components that contribute to the value perceived by the customer:

**Product Functionality**

The product or service must meet or exceed customer expectations. For example, a software that improves productivity may have a high WTP due to the efficiency it brings to the user.

**Customer Experience**

The buying and usage experience is a decisive factor. A positive experience—whether it's a user-friendly website or excellent post-sale support—increases perceived value.

**Branding and Emotional Connection**

Customers who identify with the brand's values and develop an emotional relationship with it are willing to pay more. For example, Tesla customers are willing to pay a premium because they associate the brand with innovation and sustainability.

## How to capture value

Capturing value means monetizing the difference between WTP and WTS. This can be achieved through two methods:

- Increasing the perceived value to the customer, which raises WTP and allows for higher pricing.
- Reducing costs by improving working conditions, which lowers WTS and gives companies more flexibility in pricing and profit margins.

## Case Studies

### Apple: Increasing Willingness to Pay (WTP) through innovation and branding

Apple has successfully increased WTP by focusing on innovation and creating a strong emotional connection with customers. Their products offer not only high functionality but also a premium experience in terms of design, user-friendliness, and integration into the Apple ecosystem.

### Seamless integration across devices

Apple has created an ecosystem of devices that work perfectly together, such as the iPhone, Mac, iPad, and Apple Watch. This integration allows users to switch between devices seamlessly, for example, answering calls on their Mac or iPad that were initially made to their iPhone, or sharing files easily through AirDrop. This tight ecosystem enhances convenience and creates a unique user experience that competitors find hard to replicate, significantly increasing the perceived value and WTP.

### Premium design and User Experience (UX)

Apple products are known for their sleek, minimalist design and user-friendly interface. The focus on aesthetics and usability is a core part of the Apple brand, from the packaging to the physical products themselves. This attention to detail appeals to customers who are willing to pay more for a premium, beautifully designed product that also functions intuitively. The macOS and iOS interfaces, for instance, are designed to be easy to use, even for non-technical users, making Apple devices accessible and attractive to a wide range of customers.

**Strong branding and emotional appeal**

Apple has cultivated a brand identity that is closely associated with innovation, status, and creativity. Their marketing campaigns, like the iconic "Think Different" campaign, have positioned Apple as a brand for innovators and forward-thinkers. This emotional appeal makes customers feel part of an exclusive group, increasing brand loyalty and the amount they are willing to pay. Owning an Apple product is often seen as a status symbol, which adds intangible value to the product, allowing Apple to maintain premium pricing.

**Patagonia: Decreasing Willingness to Sell (WTS) through sustainability and employee well-being**

Patagonia, the outdoor clothing and gear company, has successfully decreased WTS by focusing on environmental sustainability and creating a company culture that values employee well-being. They offer their employees good working conditions, flexibility, and meaningful work related to environmental conservation.

## Commitment to environmental sustainability

Patagonia is known for its strong environmental stance, and this is reflected in every aspect of their business. They use sustainable materials in their products, and they encourage customers to repair and reuse products instead of buying new ones, with initiatives like the Worn Wear program. This commitment not only aligns with employee values but also fosters loyalty among staff who share these principles. Employees are proud to work for a company that prioritises the planet, reducing their WTS by making them more engaged and loyal without demanding higher wages.

## Work-life balance and employee well-being

Patagonia offers a range of work-life balance benefits, including flexible working hours and access to on-site childcare. They promote a company culture that values employee well-being and health, which contributes to a positive working environment. By investing in employees' health and happiness, Patagonia has managed to retain talent without the need to constantly raise salaries or face high employee turnover, thus lowering WTS.

**Opportunities for professional development**

Patagonia encourages employees to develop professionally and provides resources for ongoing training and development. They offer opportunities for employees to attend educational programs or gain new skills, which helps reduce WTS by increasing job satisfaction. Employees feel they are growing within the company, making them more likely to stay, even without substantial salary increases.

**Lessons from Apple and Patagonia**

Apple increased Willingness to Pay (WTP) by enhancing the customer experience and creating a strong emotional connection through its innovative products and ecosystem.

Patagonia decreased Willingness to Sell (WTS) by creating a supportive work environment and promoting values that resonate with employees and customers alike.

# Growing the business through efficiency and innovation

Productivity. Productivity is not necessarily measured by the number of units produced, but rather by how efficiently customers are served and the value delivered to them. Every hour of work your team invests should contribute to creating a superior customer experience or improving the internal efficiency of your company's processes. Thus, successful businesses focus not only on the volume of activity but also on how they can offer more value per customer over time.

**Economies of Scale and the Learning Curve**

Economies of scale and the learning curve are key concepts not just in manufacturing but also in service industries. They play a critical role in reducing costs and increasing efficiency as the business grows.

**Economies of Scale**

Economies of scale refer to the phenomenon where, as a company increases the volume of services offered, the cost per unit tends to decrease. In services, this can be achieved by optimising processes, automating administrative tasks, or efficiently delegating work. For example, a consultant who automates invoicing and reporting processes can serve more clients without expanding their team, thereby increasing productivity per employee.

Additionally, as the business grows, fixed costs such as marketing are spread across a larger number of clients, reducing the cost per client. This means that the larger the company becomes, the easier it is to offer competitive prices while maintaining high profit margins.

**Learning Curve**

The learning curve is another fundamental concept. As teams become more efficient in performing repetitive tasks, the time and cost per task decrease. The more frequently a company delivers a service, the better it becomes at executing it. Thus, long-term average costs decrease, and efficiency increases.

For instance, a consulting firm that implements software for automating invoicing and project management can significantly increase its workload without hiring additional staff. Through economies of scale and efficient time use, the company can serve more clients with the same resources. Additionally, as consultants perform the same tasks for multiple clients, the learning curve improves service delivery speed and quality.

**Amazon's Logistics efficiency**

A prime example of how economies of scale and the learning curve can be applied to services is Amazon, particularly in their logistics and fulfilment operations.

**Economies of Scale in Amazon's logistics**

**Massive infrastructure investments**

Amazon has built one of the largest and most advanced logistics networks in the world, with hundreds of fulfilment centres and distribution hubs globally. Amazon reduces the cost per item handled by increasing the volume of products moving through these centres. The company's investment in automating warehouses with robotics and AI-driven inventory management systems has further optimised operations, allowing Amazon to handle a high volume of orders with fewer human resources.

**Amazon Prime Membership model**

The introduction of Amazon Prime, which offers free two-day shipping for members, is a key strategy leveraging economies of scale. As the Prime membership base grows, Amazon can offer faster, more reliable shipping at a lower incremental cost, further driving customer loyalty and increasing Willingness to Pay (WTP) for its services.

**Supplier and vendor relationships**

Amazon's vast scale also allows it to negotiate better terms with suppliers and vendors, reducing its Willingness to Sell (WTS) for products. By using its size and influence, Amazon can demand lower prices or better terms from its suppliers, which helps reduce overall costs. This cost reduction is passed on to customers through lower prices or faster service, creating a positive feedback loop where customers are willing to pay more for convenience while suppliers are willing to sell at lower margins because of the massive exposure Amazon provides.

**Learning Curve in Amazon's Operations**

**Continuous improvement in fulfilment efficiency**

Over time, Amazon has fine-tuned its fulfilment processes. From order picking to packaging, the company has continually optimised how orders are processed through its system. The introduction of Kiva robots in warehouses has drastically reduced the time required to move goods around, while machine learning algorithms forecast demand and optimise inventory management, reducing waste and out-of-stock items. As these systems become more efficient, Amazon lowers the cost per order fulfilled, and the customer experience improves in parallel.

## Technological innovation

By consistently iterating on its technology and systems, Amazon has been able to improve how quickly and accurately orders are processed. Over time, improvements like the Amazon Dash Replenishment Service, which automates reordering of household products, and the Amazon Go stores, which eliminate checkout lines, reduce friction in the customer experience. These innovations create additional value for customers, raising WTP, while the internal efficiencies generate lower operational costs.

## Dynamic Route Optimization

For Amazon's vast network of deliveries, the learning curve plays a crucial role in optimising routes for its delivery drivers. Amazon's AI-driven route planning systems learn from past deliveries to predict the most efficient routes, saving time and fuel costs. As these systems improve, they contribute to lowering the overall cost of delivery while speeding up shipping times for customers, reinforcing Amazon's reputation for fast, reliable service.

Through both economies of scale and the learning curve, Amazon has been able to optimise its logistics operations, reduce operational costs, and offer a superior customer experience. This strategy allows them to offer competitive pricing while maintaining strong margins and continuously enhancing their services.

## Benefits of Economies of Scale and the Learning Curve

In digital businesses, where variable costs are relatively low, economies of scale can be even more pronounced. Once software is developed, the cost of replication for new users is negligible. For example, an online platform can offer the same services to thousands of users without needing significant additional resources. As the user base grows, the average cost per user decreases, making the business more profitable.

The learning curve also has a major impact on efficiency in digital businesses. As developers optimise software and fix functionality issues, the time required to introduce new features decreases. This increases efficiency and reduces long-term costs, while the value perceived by customers increases.

# How to turn ideas into profitable actions: Balanced scorecard and Value Maps

A well-formulated strategy is useless if it is not implemented correctly. What separates successful companies from those that stagnate is their ability to transform ideas into concrete actions that generate profit and create long-term value. In this chapter, we will discuss essential tools like the Balanced Scorecard and Value Maps, and how you can use them to guide your business toward success.

**Balanced Scorecard: measuring and guiding performance**

The Balanced Scorecard is a tool that helps companies track performance across multiple important dimensions. It doesn't just focus on financial metrics but also covers other critical aspects such as:

**Financial Perspective: How are we doing with revenues and profitability?**

Customer Perspective: How satisfied are our customers, and how do they perceive us in the market?

**Internal Processes Perspective: How efficient are we in delivering our products and services?**

**Learning and Growth Perspective: How do we ensure that our team is growing and adapting to market changes?**

This holistic approach allows you to track not just financial gains but also the essential aspects that contribute to long-term success.

**Value Maps: evaluating and comparing your company with competitors**

Value Maps are an essential tool for understanding how you perform compared to your competition based on various criteria that influence your customers' Willingness to Pay (WTP). WTP represents the maximum amount a customer is willing to pay for your product or service, and Value Maps show you how you stack up against competitors in terms of these factors.

In a Value Map, the vertical axis represents the main factors that drive customers' purchasing decisions. These factors, called value drivers, might include aspects such as:

Price: Value for money is often crucial.

Quality: The perceived quality of your product or service.

Post-Sale Support: How well you support customers after the purchase.

On the horizontal axis, the Value Map shows your company's performance in relation to each of these factors compared to the competition. This analysis helps you identify your strengths and weaknesses and prioritise investments to maximise your customers' WTP.

**How to use Value Maps to gain a competitive advantage**

Let's assume you own an online electronics store. You can use a Value Map to assess your business performance compared to other stores based on criteria such as:

**Competitive Pricing**

Compare your prices with competitors and identify if you need to adjust your pricing strategy.

**Website Usability**

If customers find the shopping experience on your website more difficult than on competitors' sites, this is an area to focus on.

**Delivery Time**

If your product delivery takes longer than the competition, you need to invest in improving logistics.

Transitioning from strategy to execution: essential steps

Once you have identified the critical values and key factors through Balanced Scorecard and Value Maps, it's time to turn this information into concrete actions.

**Here are some essential steps for ensuring efficient strategy execution:**

### Identify the activities that need improvement

Identify internal processes that need optimization to support your strategy. For example, if you decide to invest in improving your website's user experience, start by reviewing its design and functionality.

### Assign responsibilities

Ensure that each team member knows what they need to do to support the strategy. Responsibilities should be clear and measurable.

### Allocate the necessary resources

Every project requires time, money, and personnel. Allocate the necessary resources to support the implementation of the strategy.

Set performance Indicators (KPIs) - Measure the success of each project through specific performance indicators. For example, you can track the increase in online conversions after improving the website.

# How to lower employees' willingness to sell to reduce costs

Lowering employees' Willingness to Sell (WTS) is essential for maximising productivity and reducing costs. WTS refers to the minimum compensation level an employee is willing to accept to perform their job. To maintain low costs and keep employees motivated, companies need to create a work environment that attracts and retains employees, thus reducing their desire to seek other opportunities.

**Factors that influence WTS**

Compensation isn't everything. Here are several factors that can reduce WTS:

**Flexibility and Remote Work**

Strategies like improving working conditions or offering flexible schedules reduce WTS by providing employees with non-monetary benefits. For example, after the 2020 pandemic, there was a significant increase in demand for hybrid work and flexible schedules.

The option to work from home has become a critical factor in reducing WTS. Many companies did not consider these preferences until it became necessary, but research shows that flexibility is highly valued by employees.

Organisations that offer these benefits have seen a significant decrease in WTS and an increase in employee satisfaction.

**Autonomy and training**

Another effective strategy is increasing employee autonomy and engagement. For example, Zappos, known for its customer service, implemented a system where employees are encouraged to use their discretion in resolving customer issues without strict scripts or approvals. This empowerment reduced WTS as employees felt their work added value and that they could contribute directly to the company's success.

## Recognition and personal development

Employees who feel appreciated and have opportunities for professional development tend to have a lower WTS. Starbucks is a well-known example, offering employees (referred to as "partners") various career development opportunities, including educational benefits like their College Achievement Plan, which covers tuition for eligible employees. This investment in personal growth has resulted in increased employee loyalty and reduced turnover, effectively lowering WTS.

## Reducing WTS through open conversations with employees

A key aspect of reducing WTS is maintaining open communication with employees about their needs and expectations. Regular discussions about workplace satisfaction, working conditions, and development opportunities can give the company a clear vision of what can be improved to lower WTS. Additionally, implementing a system where employees can propose ideas and solutions for improving internal processes increases engagement and reduces turnover.

Microsoft has successfully used open communication to reduce WTS by conducting frequent feedback sessions with employees. Through these discussions, Microsoft gained insights into what employees valued, and by making adjustments—like increasing work flexibility and improving work-life balance—they significantly reduced WTS and increased productivity.

**Implementing tools to reduce WTS**

One effective way to lower WTS is by giving employees more control over their work environment. Unilever implemented a program where employees could personalise their benefits package to suit their individual needs. This flexibility in tailoring benefits helped reduce WTS, as employees felt that the company was accommodating their unique circumstances, leading to higher satisfaction and lower turnover.

# How to build sustainable partnerships that improve your business

Lowering the Willingness to Sell (WTS) of suppliers is an effective strategy for creating long-term, profitable, and sustainable collaboration. Suppliers, like employees, have a minimum level of compensation they are willing to accept for the goods or services they provide. If you can reduce this WTS, you can secure better prices and more favourable conditions without compromising the quality they deliver.

**Factors that influence suppliers' WTS**

**Improving supplier efficiency**

One key method of reducing WTS is by investing in the efficiency of your suppliers. When suppliers become more efficient, their costs decrease, allowing them to reduce their prices while remaining competitive. For example, Nike established a training centre in Sri Lanka, where it taught over 400 of its apparel and footwear suppliers how to apply lean production techniques to reduce costs and improve productivity.

Lean is a process improvement methodology originating from the Japanese auto industry, particularly from Toyota, which aims to eliminate waste and optimise efficiency. The core principle of lean is identifying and removing activities that do not add value in the production process or supply chain. For suppliers, implementing lean principles means optimising production, reducing processing time, minimising inventories, and improving workflow.

**Close collaboration and long-term partnerships**

Close, trusting relationships with suppliers reduce WTS. An excellent example of reducing WTS through strategic partnerships is the collaboration between Best Buy and major electronics manufacturers such as Apple.

Best Buy allowed companies like Apple to open dedicated kiosks inside its stores, reducing operational costs for Apple and other partners. These kiosks operate like mini-stores, offering a similar experience to an Apple Store but without the high costs of running a standalone retail space.

## Why is the Apple model advantageous?

### Reduced costs for Apple and other partners

Instead of opening a dedicated physical store in every location, Apple could leverage Best Buy's existing infrastructure. This reduced expenses on rent, logistics, and staffing while providing access to a wider audience. Best Buy already had an extensive geographic presence, allowing partners to reach customers who might not have visited an exclusive Apple store.

### Access to a diverse audience

The kiosks in Best Buy stores gave partners like Apple access to a broader customer base. Some customers might not have gone directly to an Apple store but were exposed to their products while shopping at Best Buy. This collaboration helped increase brand visibility and sales without increasing operational costs.

### Reduced operational risk

By partnering with Best Buy, suppliers reduced the operational risks associated with opening and maintaining their own locations, especially in areas where operating costs would have been prohibitive. In turn, Best Buy benefited from better pricing and additional marketing support from these partners, further reducing their WTS and improving commercial relationships.

**Applying this model to other businesses**

Suppose you have a startup that relies on suppliers of construction materials. To reduce their WTS, you could offer training on optimising logistics, implementing more efficient production processes, or even helping them access new markets. In the long term, this approach not only reduces WTS and costs but also strengthens collaboration, making your business more resilient to market fluctuations.

Reducing the WTS of suppliers and partners not only lowers costs but also creates a long-term competitive advantage. Through close collaborations, investments in efficiency, and long-term partnerships, companies can ensure a steady supply chain at lower costs, contributing to overall profitability growth.

# Wrap Up

## Building a sustainable and ethical business

Building a sustainable and ethical business. The true measure of an entrepreneur's success is the ability to create a business that remains relevant, durable, and capable of delivering long-term value to customers, employees, and partners. The key is to focus on striking a balance between innovation, productivity, and ethics, all centred around the customer's needs.

Putting yourself in your customer's shoes, understanding their emotions, and providing them with a high-quality experience will become the driving force behind your growth. Optimising your resources and working efficiently with suppliers and partners will ensure that your business is profitable and sustainable. And when you treat your customers and team with respect and integrity, you'll build not just a business, but a loyal and devoted community.

If you place your customers at the heart of your business and make their needs a priority, you'll see how profit naturally follows as a consequence of the value you provide.

*Remember: building a successful business means being dedicated to investing time and resources into creating an experience that stays in the minds and hearts of your customers.*

## About the Author

Raluca Vasiliu is an expert with over 15 years of experience in product management, user experience (UX), and service design. She has worked with technology companies in the United States and the UK, contributing to the growth and development of businesses exceeding $160 million in revenue.

Raluca honed her skills at prestigious institutions like Harvard Business School Online and the Nielsen Norman Group, earning certifications in business strategy and UX. With extensive experience in sectors such as SaaS, cloud technology, and artificial intelligence, she specialises in optimising customer journeys and developing strategies that enhance user experiences and drive company growth.

Raluca is known for offering clear and effective solutions. She brings her expertise in an accessible way, tailored to each client's needs, always providing reliable support and proven practices for business success.

She also provides both free mentorship via The Mentoring Club as well as private consulting services for startups and companies seeking to implement effective business strategies, including defining personas, mapping user journeys, and creating service blueprints to optimise internal processes.

Contact:

- Email: theinvisibledesign@gmail.com
- Website: www.theinvisibledesign.com

# References

- Customer Journey Mapping - Learn how to map out your customer's journey to better understand their needs and improve their experience. theinvisibledesign.com
- Service Blueprinting - Discover how service blueprints can help you optimise internal processes and enhance customer experience. - theinvisibledesign.com
- User Personas - Personas are essential tools for understanding your users and delivering better experiences. Nielsen Norman Group - nngroup.com
- Research Methodologies - Explore the best research methodologies to ensure data-driven design and decisions. Nielsen Norman Group - nngroup.com
- Willingness to Pay - A guide to understanding how much customers are willing to pay for your products and services. Harvard Business School Online - online.hbs.edu
- Willingness to Sell - Understand the balance between how much employees or suppliers are willing to accept in exchange for their labor or services. Harvard Business School Online - online.hbs.edu
- Strategy Formulation - A guide to formulating effective business strategies for long-term

success. Harvard Business School Online - Strategy Formulation - online.hbs.edu
- Value-Based Strategy - Learn how to craft value-based strategies that align with your company's goals and customer expectations. - Harvard Business School Online - online.hbs.edu
- Daniel Kahneman - Thinking, Fast and Slow - Nobel laureate Daniel Kahneman's book explores how we make decisions, with a focus on cognitive biases that influence consumer behavior. - Amazon.com
- Don Norman - Emotional Design - Don Norman's work on emotional design explains how products that evoke positive emotions create better user experiences and higher customer satisfaction. - Amazon.com
- Foucault, M. (1997). "The Genealogy of Ethics" Referenced for its discussion on the role of emotions in modern morality.